INTERSECTIONS

INTERSECTIONS

POEMS

BY

JOANNE GROWNEY

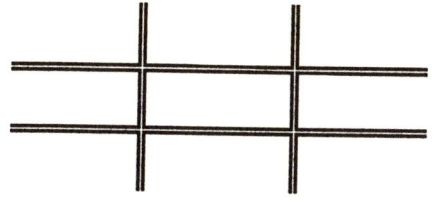

KADET PRESS

Copyright © 1993 by JoAnne Growney
All rights reserved
Printed in the United States of America

Library of Congress Catalog Card Number 93-91736
ISBN 0-9637964-0-2

Some of the poems in this book have appeared in the following publications: *Four Quarters, Carver, Scrawl, The Endless Mountain Review, The Raystown Review,* and the *Humanistic Mathematics Network Journal.* The poet extends her gratitude to the editors of these publications, first for their original publication of her work and second for the chance to publish them again here.

KADET PRESS
Bloomsburg, PA 17815-1758

Contents

I. Trees

Admiring Adda   3
A White Linen Tablecloth   4
When Daddy Died   6
Mother's Day, 1993   7
Boston Aunt   8
A Visit to Boston   9
Dream Scene   10
The Bloomsburg Fair   11
Grumblings   14

II. Clouds

My Possessions   19
Why I Limp   20
Power   21
Mourning   22
Tomorrow   23
New Year's Irresolution   24
In and Out   25
WORDS ARE BIRDS   26
Lament of a Professor . . .   27
Justice   28
Come, Spring!   30

III. BUTTERFLIES

Daily Exercise 33
Flirtation 34
Halloween 35
Quiet Time 36
Invite a Leprechaun 37
July in Bloomsburg 38
Be Quiet 38
Ask the Owl 39
I Like Spring 40
Wishes 41
Patchwork Woman 42

IV. NUMBERS

Counting 45
A Mathematician's Nightmare 46
Changing Colors 47
Misunderstanding 48
Mathematics and Poetry . . . 49
December and June 50
Orders of Magnitude 51
The Prince of Algebra 52
Expectations 54
San Antonio, January, 1993 55
You asked me for a birthday . . . 56

I

TREES

Tree at my window, window tree,
My sash is lowered when night comes on;
But let there never be curtain drawn
Between you and me.
                              Robert Frost

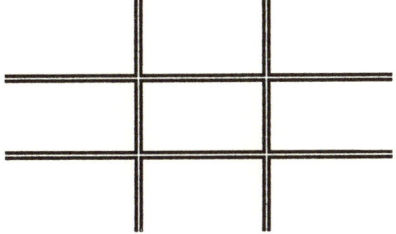

Admiring Adda

I visit her family portrait, focus
on Mother — little girl who wouldn't, couldn't
sit still, who stole the gazes of the other
four who meant to watch the camera but didn't
and have been caught forever watching Adda.
After this beginning, no surprise
that sixty-five years later, Adda still
plays center. Widowed young, she set her eyes

on the future, ran the farm, the children,
taught eighth grade, nursed Grandma. Believer
that God helps those who work hard, that women
are the stronger half. Now brother, sister

lean on her. She will never cease to use
her energy to make the world improve.

A White Linen Tablecloth

Tell me a story of you growing up,
I coaxed my aunt one day,
What were days like when Daddy was young?
Give me a picture to save.

    Meals were prompt at twelve and six
    on a stiff white linen cloth,
    a clean one spread each Saturday night
    to honor the coming Sabbath.

    Each of us sat up straight,
    cut one bite at a time.
    Dinner at noon was eat-and-run,
    supper had conversation.

    Father called on each to give
    an interesting report
    of day's events.
    I was youngest, always last.

    I ate carefully trying not
    to dribble jam to mark my spot
    'til Saturday, (or Wednesday,
    when Mother reversed the cloth).

    Father honored Mother dear
    by hiding his dribbles with coins —
    a dime or nickel, once a half-dollar,
    for her to spend on neverminds.

Life on the farm
was neither sad nor merry —
always busy, and respectful
of white linen.

When Daddy Died

All I could do
was milk the cow,
leaning close for comfort,
filling the pail with white tears.

Mother's Day, 1993

> Let not your heart be troubled: ye believe in
> God, believe also in me. In my Father's house
> are many mansions: if it were not so, I would
> have told you. I go to prepare a place for you.
> *St. John*, 14, 1-2.

I wave goodbye but do not let you go.
Tomorrow you'll be seated in your chair,
and I'll decide what is and isn't so.

Though death will finish me, I want to know
that your belief has paid your way somewhere.
I wave goodbye but do not let you go.

Roads to the next life fork to hell below.
I'd send each straight-and-narrow zealot there --
except for you. I don't condemn you so.

Your absence makes me doubt the things I know.
I want a sign from heaven that you're there.
I wave goodbye but do not let you go.

Jumbled and lonely, I waver to and fro.
My hands move with your gestures trying prayer.
Would you have told me that which isn't so?

Alive, you tried to rule, while I said No.
Bereft of your dominion, I'm unsure.
I wave goodbye but cannot let you go.
Would you have told me things that are not so?

Boston Aunt

When my sister goes to heaven
she will organize the angels
to move apace around that place
and to delight in the sight
and sound and taste of paradise
even more than before.

Though some may think she won her crown
by retaining human nature
in a corporate jungle,
insiders know
the practice that made her perfect
came from aunthood.

Gracious host for summer camp
in her tiny condominium,
director of sightseeing tours.
"Today we'll march the Freedom Trail
to discover history."
"Did you ever see a shark?
Come to the Aquarium."
"Ever ride a subway?
We'll take the T."
On to Fenway Park,
to Science Museum, encouraging
tired legs to walk another step.
"Let's eat at Quincy Market.
I'll buy, if you'll try something new."

"Follow me to take a giant step
over the horizon of your home town."

A Visit to Boston

I like the looks on faces of country boys
who walk down Boylston Street and see Trinity
Church reflected perfectly in Hancock Tower.
These restless boys slow for a swan boat ride
and stroll through flower gardens. They behave
with reverence in Old North Church and smile
through dinner with parents at Durgin Park,
politely recounting day's events,
betraying no signs of the arrogant
independence that they routinely wear
at home in a small town.

Dream Scene

Each tree beside the parking lot
bows low. Today no ordinary
clan reunion for inspection
of babies and tales of yesteryear.
Beethoven's heroic symphony
is in the air. A score of people stroll,
nod, see me not. Father looks tall
with Mother on his arm and she is
beautiful in ways I never knew.
My uncle in his uniform wears gaiety
that he'll soon lose in Germany. My aunts
are ladies each, full of chatter
concerning fashion, men, and books. I want
to know them with these youthful ways.

The Bloomsburg Fair

In September,
the Bloomsburg Fair.
I escape my scorn
for dirt and crowds
and hurry there
to taste each scent —
sausages, funnel cakes,
Mongolian barbecue, candied popcorn.

I'm fascinated
by the exhibits.
A giant pumpkin —
three-hundred-forty-five pounds,
not round, more like a bean-bag chair.
How did Anna Stolfus
make it grow so large?
How did she lift it
to bring it here?

A team of guessers,
Myrtle and John,
take dollar after dollar
from gamblers who suppose
they look a different age.
Myrtle peers deep
into a bettor's eyes,
then guesses on the nose.
Mistaken once. A midlife couple
asked the number of their wedded years.
Though Myrtle said "Eleven,"
it was "One." A missing digit.
Two years back,
when Mother was seventy-eight,
John guessed, "Seventy-three."
"Kind to old folks," Mother said.

All night the Midway glows and roars.
I pause beside the Scrambler.
Now or later I'll give in and pay
three dollars for three minutes of excited prayer
to escape alive from spinning there.

Whack-A-Mole's my favorite game.
Quick, quick, beat the clock,
beat the other players.
Pound the darting plastic varmint —
win another candy dish.

In front of side-show tents,
a barker barks his come-on-ins.
Why don't my students receive theorems
as willingly as passersby
accept his lies?

Once I paid to see "The Smallest Horse
in the Universe," declared as "Under
Twenty Inches High." On a platform
beside its flank, I stood with less
than twenty inches of horse above my feet.
I expected a more-clever fraud.

Each year the Bloomsburg Fair
celebrates the truth with lies.
If parallels will never meet —
then here's a man with snakes for hair,
and there's a woman with three eyes.

Grumblings

*A verse to be said with lavish vocal expression
and with many hugs and tickles.*

I look back and see
the knotting of our family ties
in the back seat
of our station wagon.

Trips with our four kids
lead to little grumblings —
  *How far to go? I can't see.
  I have a headache. He hit me.*
With three hundred miles of road ahead,
Wallace frowns and shakes his head,
JoAnne dutifully climbs to the back
to start the entertainment.

The mother's place is the middle,
straddling the hump, feeling each bump.
K and T have window seats,
E and D get lap.

  Take a deep breath, Mother —
  forget the fact
  that travel might
  give time for meditation
  or front-seat conversation.
  Mother's place
  is back there
  to deal with grumbling in the air.
  Rhyming stories are the mode
  to keep kids happy on the road.

K and T and E and D
were known as "The Four Little Grumblings."
Start with me, Mom,
start with me!
You know we do the oldest first,
K then T then E then D.
Let's see. We're on our way —
the oldest Grumbling girl was K.

K was sugar, K was spice,
K was everything that's nice.
Mistress K, bright and gay,
how does your garden grow today?

Here's an old woman
in a shoe
with so many children —
what will she do?

T, T, the piper's son,
got a pig and had some fun.
He fed, he scrubbed, he played with her,
She was known as his "porker."

Hickory, dickory, dock,
E wound up the clock.
The clock struck one, but E
didn't hear it — E was asleep.

I have a little shadow
that goes in and out with me.
She's a cuddly little shadow,
and her name is D.

K and T went up the hill
to fetch a pail of water.
They liked the view up there
and called for E and D to come.

Four blind mice, four blind mice —
see how they grumble, see how they grump,
Did you ever see such a sight?
Shall we cut off their tales?

Old Mother Cole was a merry old soul,
a merry old soul was she.
She called for K and she called for T,
she called for E and for Princess D.

These four fiddlers did a fine fiddle,
a very fine fiddle they did.
Then — at last — they collapsed,
tired of fiddling.

"Since I am King," said old Mother Cole,
"Since I am King," said she.
"I proclaim the next five minutes
to be silent. Shhhhhhh."

II

CLOUDS

I wandered lonely as a cloud
That floats on high o'er vales and hills . . .
              William Wordsworth

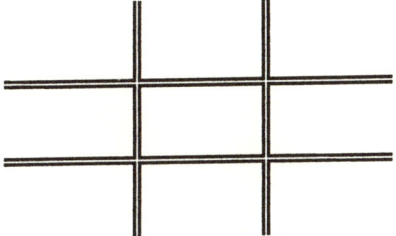

My Possessions

I have
good health,
a good mind,
good luck,

and worry —
that my words
seem foolish
to you.

Why I Limp

I put a pebble
in my shoe,
to change my pace
to walk with you.

Power

We danced in circles on hot sand
and wished ourselves on peaks that sat
less than a day away.

Suddenly he fled
to an oasis
that I imagined
he imagined.

Alone, I knew the desert's burn.
I survived -- with half a heart,
my strength does not return.
With fragile arms I hug my child,
my eyes see now that blades of grass
are beautiful and smiles are warm.

When he returns and dances
on the roof of my garage,
I toss my head and banish him
into a mirage.

Mourning

So easy to lose things
I didn't know I had --
a pleasant disposition,
a quiet friend.

Late night.
I hear snow flakes
land on seed pods
of my neighbor's mimosa tree.

Tomorrow

        When I drive on country
roads I look for stones heaped up as walls.
I like the practicality
of using rocks from fields

        to fence the very fields
in which they rose to halt a plow
in spring. In my garage lie boards
that once stood in a row

        and were my backyard fence.
Now I select them one by one
to border flower beds. I glance
ahead toward death — if stone

        and wood receive new homes,
I'm satisfied that flesh and bones
will fare no worse. Assured, I sigh —
I also will not die.

New Year's Irresolution

Holiday stress, unwelcome guest —
have a piece of apple pie.
I'd go south, if I could fly.

It's New Year's Day and I will play,
for if I work, it's work I'll do
each day the whole year through.

What to do but work, when kids are grown
and all alone I don't want drink
and cannot think of who to phone.

I want to hold a hand,
although I know that life's a bore
if what I get is what I want.

In and Out

Tired and thin,
I'm winding down.
Soon my search will end —
I'll find Anita Brown
and jump inside her skin.
We'll both leave town.

WORDS ARE BIRDS

TRASH IS CASH

                I saw a bumper sticker
                while I was carrying

HEALTH IS WEALTH

                her worn belongings
                to an auction site

REST IS BEST

                where they were sold
                to help my aunt

AGE IS CAGE

                pay her way into
                a nursing home to die.

Lament of a Professor
at the End of the Spring Semester

I took an extra step to bridge the gap
between us, blind to your matching backward step.
We've moved in tandem until I'm angry
at you, and at me — I thought you needed
lenience, but my obstinance instead
would have changed the direction of our cadence
and given you a chance to lead the dance.

Justice

Monday

Officer, come here, arrest
this bum. He spit on my silk
blouse. *Show me the spot, madam.*
There ain't foodstuff in that spit.
He hain't eaten. Did he beg
you for a coin for food? Yes,
of course, he always does, but
I am not responsible
for him. *Yes, madam, you are.*

Tuesday

Hello, Precinct Fifty-one,
come now, arrest the creature
who sleeps on cardboard outside
my boutique. I must arouse
her putrid presence every
morning when I open up.
Madam, I gotta ask you,
did she beg you for a job?
Of course, repeatedly, but
I said No. She's gross. I'm not
responsible for the likes
of her. *Yes, madam, you are.*

Wednesday

Officer, you are unjust.
Why are you arresting me?
Tell me the charge. My failure
to obey the golden rule?
Surely you joke. I always
stand alone on my two feet,
expect the same of others.
Madam, you have just confessed.
It's my duty to arrest.

Come, Spring!

Not all frogs are princes, but some
have royal lineage, and I can cut
the gloom of a December afternoon,
if I remember that. Yesterday
winter held Pennsylvania by the throat.
Grim at my desk I sat biting

my pencil, wanting something to match
the curves of my body better
than my leather chair, something
to hug more tightly than my long
red coat. My son said, Get a dog.
No good. I am done with mothering.

Hurry, spring, come and surprise me
with blue violets beneath
the tamarack, with croaking frogs
awaking from hibernation
in soft mud. When I greet
and kiss them, I will find a prince.

III

BUTTERFLIES

Will your worms become part
of dogs or of butterflies?
> Pablo Neruda
> XXXVI, *The Book of Questions*

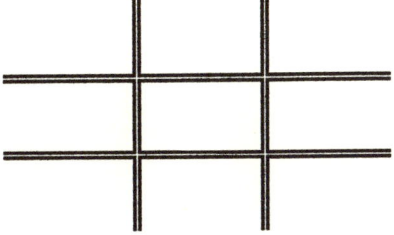

Daily Exercise

One of my favorite spots
to jog is the old dusty
warm-up track at the Fairground.
Sometimes I share that circle
with trainers in their sulkies
urging sturdy Standard-breds.
On sandy sod my feet start
slowly, then gain speed until
my chestnut mane lifts and floats.
My tail streaks out behind.

My gallop drives me outside
the turning track, across the field.
I cross traffic, not hearing
auto horns, not feeling stares
from bystanders —— scoffers left
behind in the world I conquer
when my imagination spends
the energy no longer needed
for the trip back home,
which is no longer house.

Flirtation

One warm March day
I was at the curb
washing my car
with a bucket and sponge.

He came down his front steps
and called across,
"How much would you charge
to wash mine?"

"A hundred dollars," I replied.
"Goodness," said he, "Water's high-priced
on your side of the street."
"Not so," I bantered, "It's labor that's dear."

Again, three months later,
he came out of his house
while I was scrubbing my car.
"I can't afford a car wash,

but I could take you
out to dinner," he offered.
"Perhaps," I responded,
"Where would we go?"

Halloween

Oak leaves dance
in candlelight
from Jack-o'-lantern's smile.

Scarecrows dress in lies
and red and blue striped ties
to campaign for reelection.

Witches sit in kitchens
and brew complaints, but don't
register to vote.

Bigots call for reformation,
hiding their black hearts
under ghostly garments.

Oak leaves fall.
Darkness comes earlier
today than yesterday.
Mischief dances
in Jack-o'-lantern's candlelight.

Quiet Time

Peter doesn't like to cut
the lawn. Still, he always asks
why I did it, not waiting
till he found time. Embarrassed,
he says it's man's work, neighbors
will think hard of him, of me.
Tell them I like to mow, I say.

I like to start the mower —
quick jerk of cord requiring
timing, defying strength.
First, trim around the corner
maple, circle clothes-line posts,
the lilac bush. Carve a rectangle.
Now mowing is contentment.

Lean forward, push — straight a while,
then neatly turn. No phone calls
ring loud enough to interrupt
the motor's roar. I don't hear children
call for lemonade. Butterflies
dance for my machine. I let go
thoughts I have no need to think
and find a poem.

Invite a Leprechaun

Why weren't the doors left open?

Happiness needs
good luck
through an open door.

Magic lives
between us —
not inside.
Stand nearby
to make me sure.

When leaves show their undersides
in love with the breeze,
open the door.

July in Bloomsburg

August heat sat down,
spread her heavy skirts around,
and stayed, stayed, stayed, stayed.

Be Quiet

I scream at the birds
who ignore my rule
for Sunday morning silence.

Ask the Owl

who can distinguish
who is wise and
who is fool and
who is merely malcontent

who can tell
who will stay and
who will flee and
who will pay the rent

I Like Spring

In May I look for
long legs, sandals,
bouncing gaits,
short skirts,
and

arms tanned by sunshine,
lilac perfume,
long red nails —
catch that
hand.

Wishes

Wishes are horses.
Rhythm and rhyme
are the echoes of wishes
racing through time.

Horses are lovers
in need of a beat,
a plan, a routine,
a schedule to meet.

Lovers are beggars
in search of a tryst
where horses are wishes
and ride to the west.

namoW krowhctaP Patchwork Woman

,eldeeN Needle,
,daerht etihW White thread,
mahgnig der fo parcS Scrap of red gingham,
gnikrow regnif desuollaC Calloused finger working
suoituac ,sehctits nevE Even stitches, cautious
thgirb fo rennalP Planner of bright
,retliuq ,sngiseD Designs, quilter,
.tliuQ Quilt.

IV

NUMBERS

Where there is number,
there is beauty.
Proclus

Counting

God made the integers, all else is man's
invention, said Kronecker, but I
prefer the Biblical account,
where God made one and just one
more. Dissatisfied with
only one and two,
woman and man
began the
chain to
more.

One
added
forever,
joined by zero,
matched by opposites,
sets up the integers,
base for construction of more
new numbers from old — ratios,
radical roots and transcendentals,
transfinite cardinals — mathematics bold!

A Mathematician's Nightmare

Suppose a general store —
items with unknown values
and arbitrary prices,
rounded for ease to
whole-dollar amounts.

Each day Madame X,
keeper of this emporium,
raises or lowers each price —
exceptional bargains
and anti-bargains.

Even-numbered prices
divide by two,
while odd ones climb
by half themselves —
then half a dollar more
to keep the numbers whole.

Today I pause before
a handsome beveled mirror
priced at twenty-seven dollars.
Shall I buy or wait
for fifty-nine long days
until the price is lower?

This poem's price-changing scheme comes from an unsolved problem, the Collatz Conjecture: start with any positive integer — if it is even, cut it in half; if odd, increase it by half and round up to the next whole number. Collatz' Conjecture asserts that, for any starting number, iteration of this increase-decrease process eventually leads to one.

Changing Colors

Blue
yoyo —
awkwardly
stopping-starting,
rising-plummeting,
seeking self-control. Please,
mother-friend-lover-child, don't
pull string. Let me collect myself.

I lift myself to the treetops,
soar with the golden eagle,
find rest on fleecy clouds.
My orb embraces
everybody —
powerful,
yellow
sun.

In this poem, as in several others in this collection, the numbers of syllables in consecutive lines are consecutive positive integers. Here we have 1-2-3-4-5-6-7-8–8-7-6-5-4-3-2-1.

Misunderstanding

Ah, you are a mathematician,
    they say with admiration
    or scorn.

Then, they say,
    I could use you
    to balance my checkbook.

I think about checkbooks.
    Once in a while
    I balance mine,
    just like sometimes
    I dust high shelves.

Mathematics and Poetry Are Beautiful

Each one I meet I ask, "Do you
find mathematics beautiful
or useful?" All answer, "Useful.
I use math every day." My eyes
reveal that I want proof, and each
goes on to tell that she subtracts
to keep her checkbook, and sometimes
multiplies to find the size
of carpet for the dining room.

If I, instead, would say, "Do you
find beauty or utility
in poetry?" would each person say,
"It's useful. I use it every day."
For proof would she go on to tell
that rhymes help her remember
the number of days each month —
like "Thirty hath September" —
and spellings of words with "i" and "e."

Someday utilitarians
will join with me to see
beauty in mathematics —
and in poetry.

December and June

                    cold
                 winds howl
                geese go south
             nights long   June waits
             temperatures fall low
           ponds freeze   snowmen grow
          toboggans slide down hillsides
          sun hides   ice coats   June waits
            wood-fires flame   snowballs fly
          winds howl   groundhogs hibernate

            sun glows   raspberries ripen
             catbird sings   iris blooms
        days bright   streams play   June dreams
            holiday picnics catch flies
             wheat thrives   crickets chirp
                tomato plants climb
              streams dance   June plays
                  catbird sings
                    sun glows
                      warm

The numbers of syllables in the phrases of this poem follow the patterns of factorization of the integers from 1 to 10, then 10 to 1, into prime factors. For example, line six has phrases of lengths two syllables and three syllables, using the factorization 6 = 2 × 3. Line eight has three phrases with two syllables, using 8 = 2 × 2 × 2.

Orders of Magnitude

        Union wages motivate
thousands of workers in lines to assemble
millions of Fords, but what price persuades
trillions of atoms to hold hands together
            to form the George Washington Bridge?

The Prince of Algebra

Madam Professor,
Let me introduce myself —
I'm Albert James,
whom you may know
by my test score
that's lower than my age.

Your algebra tests
are too long for me
in fifty minutes,
but I am proud
of my attendance —
I never miss class,
never come late.

I am preparing
for a new career.
For thirty years I was
with the Postal Service,
never absent,
never late.

Your mathematics
is important!
It runs the clock
which runs the mail.
Now I train to be
a first grade teacher.

I will teach
mathematics
by punctuality
and perfect attendance.

Expectations

Don't let mathematics
teach you to expect two
to be more than one.

It's sad but true that two
can get too near,
can interfere,
can reduce each other
to less than one,
to less than half.

Don't let mathematics
teach you to expect one
to be the sum of its parts.

One hour is time enough
to read the paper
or eat lunch,
but sixty minutes
are sixty times too small
for anything but frustration.

San Antonio, January, 1993

A mathematician left the convention
focused on 9, the digit that sits
in the billionth decimal place of π,
ratio of circumference to width
of the yellow circle that parted
the clouds as she strolled down Commerce Street
to a Tex-Mex café for lunch and a beer.

On fire with jalapeños
she went shopping
for a souvenir.
She bought earrings —
red-red plastic peppers
with green stems.

She said, "A hot pepper
is like my mathematics —
with strong flavor
that takes over
whatever
it enters."

You asked me
for a birthday gift suggestion . . .

No, not a sable coat, nor diamond ring,
I want a gift that doesn't cost a dime
or a life. Offer me a magic thing.
Find me a number, perhaps a prime —
to check my tendency to subdivide
myself. Avoid digits like two and five
whose familiarity weakens magic.
Give me an emblem to wear on my T-shirt.
Perhaps I'd like a big red seventeen,
a bold insignia that's not a bit obscene
and shows up on the calendar each month to say
that I am more than half-way through the days
I count, in search of truth mixed with a dream
of August picnics and homemade peach ice cream.